The Womb Diaries

[signature]

Find me on Amazon!

email - authorsmcrawford@gmail.com

The Womb Diaries

By

Sabrina Michelle Crawford

Cover art by Kozakura @ fiverr.com/kozakura

Edited by Shantell E. Jamison

To: My first loss that I initially didn't have the courage to name, my second loss Chloé and my Rainbow Baby Connor.

For every woman that has experienced this type of loss and then felt lost, this is for you. This is for us.

When do you remember having your first diary? Maybe it was a regular notebook. Maybe it was a little fancy with that small, generic lock and key that EVERY journal had. Regardless of what you used, that diary contained your most intimate thoughts, your wildest dreams, and the parts of you that no one else was trusted enough to see. I protected my diaries with my life because they contained my life! The pages of my diary understood me when nobody else could or did.

So, what are *The Womb Diaries*? Our wombs are the very essence of what make us "women." They contain the blueprints of life. They contain history. They contain the story of us, but what happens when our story takes a devastating turn? Or when things don't go according to plan? What do we do with the pieces when we have literally been broken? In *The Womb Diaries*, we will sit face-to-face with our experiences of miscarriage in its various forms, including stillbirth.

These pages will be where we can discuss our experiences in a safe space as we address our shadow side—the side of us that is hidden and suppressed—although it heavily affects what we think, say, and do. Our shadow side is always with us and normally contains parts of us that need to be addressed and/or healed. *The Womb Diaries* are meant to help guide you through some of those spaces. These diary pages are yours. No judgements. No expectations.

Since we are on this journey to healing together, I want to share my experiences of miscarrying with you.

I remember the first time I found out I was pregnant. I'd become so drained and fatigued and I couldn't figure out why. Then came the chest soreness and I immediately thought to myself, "I think I'm pregnant." I took a test and sure enough, I was. Being pregnant for the first time allowed fear to envelope me, but I still somehow immediately went into Mommy mode. I made an appointment to visit the Women's Center to confirm my pregnancy and get more information. I wondered what the baby might look like, what kind of mom I would be, and what names I would perhaps choose from.

I remember laying down to have an ultrasound on the day of my first appointment. I knew I wasn't that far along, and was excited to finally get to see my baby and get more information. I found out that I was about 7 weeks. I saw baby. So tiny. So vulnerable. We looked for a heartbeat ...and looked ...and listened ... and looked, but couldn't find one. All those thoughts and dreams I had were sucked into this black hole in the atmosphere. I immediately began to question myself. I questioned my worth as a woman.

I wondered what was wrong with my body; I criticized myself for EVERY action. Did I not sleep enough? Did I walk too much? Did I lift something that was too heavy? Was my shower temperature too hot? Were the vitamins that I took not what I needed?

I cried.
And cried.
And cried.

All I could replay in my mind was the ultrasound and the silence in the room when I didn't hear a heartbeat. All I could relive was how my heart IMMEDIATELY stopped beating. If I could've given my baby the life of my heartbeat, I would've with no hesitation. I lost a part of me that day and spent time trying to put the pieces of myself back together.

Trying to navigate my daily routine as if nothing happened was one of the hardest things I ever had to do. How did I fall in love so fast with someone I had never met and never seen? Only a few people had known that I was pregnant. Outside of them, it was a secret. The loneliness and mental torture that came with acting as if everything was normal was utterly painful. I was an actress that wore a smile on my face every day, moving about and navigating through the world. I was in my body, but I wasn't myself. I didn't know who I was anymore, but eventually, I got "better." I use quotation marks because I wasn't truly "better." I was just able to manage.

Then it happened again the very next year, but this time it was more extreme. When I found out I was pregnant, I was terrified! When an at-home pregnancy test confirmed that I was pregnant, I kept the news to myself for a few days before I told my husband at the time. Once again, I went into Mommy mode while counting down the days until I made it to 14 weeks since that's the point where the risk of miscarriage drops significantly. The pregnancy started off normal. When I had my first ultrasound there was a wave of relief that came over me as I saw and heard my baby's heartbeat – priceless. I started to feel more and more confident.

Around week 10, I began to bleed almost nonstop and decided to go into the doctor. It was the first doctor's visit of many. Every time we looked, my baby appeared to be okay. Some women just experience bleeding during their pregnancy.

However, I noticed that my pregnancy symptoms were extreme: extreme fatigue, extreme sensitivity to light, an extreme aversion to food to name a few. My body could barely function. I would walk so slow, and it appeared as if I was moving in slow motion. Even then, I would need to pause and take breaks. My job at the time was a 10-minute walk from the train to the my employer's office building downtown. The walk took 30 minutes in the state I was in. Yet and still, baby looked fine. I was about 15 weeks along and after complaining about the bleeding again, I went back into the doctor's office. The ultrasound showed baby, but she—gender was never confirmed, but I felt it was a girl—wasn't really moving. The practitioner nudged my belly and baby moved, but she moved very slowly. I felt something wasn't right, but I had made it past the highest point of miscarriage risk, right?

A couple of days later, things took a turn for the worse again. I miscarried my baby in one of the worst ways imaginable. After getting to the hospital and confirming that the baby was indeed gone, I went home. I wanted to die. Still, something wasn't right. I kept vomiting, was short of breath, dizzy, and felt like fainting. I asked my mom, younger brother and his daughter to come be with me.

I was back in the same dark space that was all too familiar, and I was completely broken.

Again, I cried.
And cried.
And cried.

How did I leave the house that morning carrying life and return home with nothing?! All I could keep saying to my Brother was, "I lost her." I somehow found a way to sleep that night, but early that morning, I was awakened due to feeling sicker than the night before. I knew I needed to get to the ER.

Upon arrival at the hospital, testing was done and all of a sudden it turned into all hands on deck as a medical team swarmed around and over me. We ended up discovering that I somehow ended up with a blood infection, which caused me to miscarry and was about to take my life as well. I will spare the details that ensued, but it was one of the most terrifying experiences. I wouldn't wish it on anyone. The end result was me staying in the hospital for two weeks. The only way I could be sent home was to have a pic-line inserted in my arm to go across my chest internally, over my heart to drip medicine 24 hours a day, for another two weeks.

I plummeted back into that dark space, but this time much deeper than before.
"WHAT IS WRONG WITH ME?!"
"I AM NOT A WOMAN!"
"WHY CANT MY BODY DO WHAT IT WAS CREATED TO DO?!"

I put the blame all on myself again. Did I eat something wrong? Did I touch something I shouldn't have touched? Did I get too stressed? Did I use a cleaning chemical I shouldn't have used?! The depression got worse. I no longer wanted to be here. I couldn't sustain life. I felt ugly. I felt low. I felt like I had let both of my babies down. I tried apologizing to my second loss as I saw her in my dreams, while I once again packed away the hopes, dreams, and brief memories. What made things more difficult this time was the fact that my pregnancy was much more public. More people knowing meant more questions about what happened. Even though there was genuine concern, each conversation reopened the wound.

A couple of years later, I got pregnant again.

Despite my marriage at the time not being in a good place, we were able to welcome a beautiful, healthy baby boy. Though baby made it safely to our arms, the amount of fear and anxiety I had was insurmountable, especially because I didn't discover I was pregnant until I was about 2 months along. I had to force-feed myself positive thoughts, which was immensely hard given the circumstances surrounding me.

My son is now 6. Despite time passing since my losses, I can assuredly confirm that they have permanently changed me. I am not the same person, nor will I ever again be. Miscarrying in a sense robs you of a certain type of innocence.

Going through the experience of miscarriage is like dealing with a delicate item, perhaps a vase or treasured figurine that's been passed down from generation to generation. It gets knocked over and breaks, so out comes the glue to attempt to put it back together. The item is repaired, but is it ever truly the same? Often there are cracks, lines, or missing pieces. Some of the pieces may be a totally different color or material, because something random was used to patch up a spot that otherwise couldn't be repaired. Sadly, sometimes even patchwork can't help and the object is a total loss.

We are the same way. Perhaps we can be repaired, but more than likely, we'll never be the same. Tragically, some of us can't be put back together at all. I was almost that person, but I knew I needed to figure out how to begin to put my pieces back together. The process I used and STILL use is what you and I will now embark on together.

START HERE:

Before you embark on this mini journey of inner shadow work, I want you to open your mind and heart. I want you to be honest. I want you to be okay with being angry. I want you to be okay with feeling inadequate. I want you to be okay with being sad. I want you to be okay with being happy. I want you to be okay with being hopeful. Then, I NEED AND WANT YOU TO BE POWERFUL!

The Womb Diaries are meant to be a starting point on a path that so many of us have not taken for one reason or another—denial, fear, anger, sadness, etc. However, events such as the loss of a child totally change us as a person, even if we don't speak on them. Repair is imperative to rebuilding. When you suffer something extreme, the trauma alters you down to rewiring your brain.

I pray that this diary helps guide your heart and feet towards recognizing your inner beauty and strength and gaining insight towards where you might need help. *The Womb Diaries* is meant to be followed for 30 days, but by no means do you have to go in order, nor should you if you don't want to. You can go from front to back, the reverse, or close your eyes and let a page choose you. Each day comes with an affirmation for you to repeat a minimum of 3x's (or more if you wish) and questions that will take you into shadow work. Sometimes it will be messy and other times it won't, but it will all be beautiful!!!

Let's lay the foundation.

This journal explores three vital stages to walking the path of healing from the trauma of miscarriage, and they are the ones I went through myself to navigate the feelings, thoughts, and emotions that needed to be processed to begin. They are acceptance, acknowledgement and advancement. Accepting what occurred and acknowledging your feelings will be handled first. Then we will work on advancement.

Going through these emotions CAN and WILL be draining, so we will use the Pendulation Technique. This approach is used in psychology/therapy for coping with trauma. It allows us to move between being triggered by a traumatic event and a state of calm. Remember, TO HEAL, YOU HAVE TO FEEL!

There are 31 journal prompts/affirmations that you are to repeat three times to yourself. The Rule of 3 in writing is a principle that suggests that a trio of things is more likely to engage us and stick in our memories. You can say them out loud or silently—whatever makes you feel comfortable. Following the prompt/affirmation, we then explore the statement. This allows us to think deeper and access parts of us that are buried and consciously or subconsciously affect us. Each prompt will have a heart by it that you can fill in so you can bookmark a topic you may want to come back to or discuss further with your mental health professional if you have one.

Let us begin.

Acceptance & Acknowledgement

Acceptance & Acknowledgement

Webster's Dictionary definition of acceptance is: "the act of showing that you know, admit, or accept that something exists or is true." Many of us have tried to ignore or suppress the fact that we lost a baby/babies; some of us hide it even more if no one knows. Realistically, miscarriage is an extremely traumatic event. It's an occurrence that some either never recover from, or have a hard time doing so.

I will say this again and repeatedly throughout this book: TO HEAL, YOU HAVE TO FEEL! Ignoring and suppressing your feelings and things that have happened is a trauma response that leaves you stuck. Feelings need somewhere to go. They are a form of energy. Holding in raw, painful feelings affects how we feel about and manage ourselves and others. It can be surprising to realize how various parts of your life are subconsciously impacted as a result of burying or removing things from our lives that negatively affected us. Let's now accept & acknowledge.

"It has been so hurtful and heavy to carry this pain of loss." (Affirm 3xs)

My losses felt like a literal weight. A weight so heavy that it felt like too much to even hold my head or arms up. My eyes were physically heavy from so much crying, but I hated to close my eyes. Closing my eyes possibly meant sleep, and the last thing I wanted to do was sleep and potentially dream about what was going on in my life. It is okay to admit how destructive this experience has been to and for us. Use this space to talk about that pain and hurt. Let it out.

_____

_____

_____

_____

_____

_____

_____

_____

"It is okay for me to grieve." (Affirm 3xs)

Your grief is valid even if you didn't get to fully carry your baby to term. The worst thing to hear is that it "wasn't really a baby yet," or at least I "lost the child early on than further along." I thought those were the most insensitive things to say to someone. How can you diminish or try to quantify someone's pain or experience? You have every right to mourn the life that you immediately started planning for as soon as you knew you were with child. If you didn't get to grieve, what kept you from properly grieving? Was it a person? Your own thoughts? Did you ever feel guilty for grieving? If so, why? If you allowed yourself to grieve, what did you do as a part of that process?

_____
_____
_____
_____
_____
_____
_____

"Because of my loss/losses, I am angry & mad." (Affirm 3xs)

Universally, anger is a feeling that all women feel when they lose their babies. Being mad is the only feeling that I felt justified what I went through because none of the other emotions seemed to fit. Since all those other emotions were stuck, it made me even more agitated, which led to even more anger. I was mad with everyone and everything, especially myself. How angry were you when you experienced your loss? Are you still angry? Do you feel as if nobody understood why you were angry? Who were you angry at the most? Were you angry with yourself?

_____

_____

_____

_____

_____

_____

_____

_____

"I accept that I lost a baby/babies and transmute that pain to build a better and stronger version of myself." (Affirm 3xs)

It's easy to allow your traumas to consciously or subconsciously shape who you are. Being permanently altered due to a life-changing experience isn't something that we can control, but we can manage how we respond to it. By acknowledging and accepting what has happened to us and not ignoring or suppressing the experience, we get to take the energy and power back that has been attached to it. Take the negative energy and transmute it. Use the broken pieces of you to build an even better you. Do you find it hard to accept what happened to you in terms of your loss/losses? If you accepted what happened to you, do you feel like it made you weaker or stronger? How do you think you can use your experience to help others?

_____

_____

_____

_____

_____

"I did not fail my baby/babies." (Affirm 3xs)

You did not fail your offspring. I know that's what it feels like because I felt the same way and sometimes STILL do. We can't control nature, and not understanding why or how this happened can cause us to blame ourselves. You did the best you could in the capacity that your situation allowed— even if that means there was absolutely nothing you could do. Do your loss/losses make you feel as if you failed your baby/babies? If you don't feel like a failure, do you feel as though you let your baby/babies down?

_____

"I am not a failure." (Affirm 3xs)

My body had failed to do one of the main things it was created to do—hold and birth life. What good was I? In my mind, my value as a woman lessened. I had failed the two babies that were helpless and dependent on me to bring them into this world alive. I had to stop comparing myself to other women who had successful pregnancies, because that was pushing me deeper into feeling like a failure. Do your loss/losses make you feel like a failure? Who do you feel like you failed? If you felt like a failure, is it also something that you can trace back to childhood or other experiences while growing up?

_____

_____

_____

_____

_____

_____

_____

_____

THE WOMB DIARIES ANXIETY-FREE TEA

As a person who suffers from anxiety, I am determined to find holistic ways to manage my condition and avoid prescribed medication as much as possible. This anxiety-free tea uses natural herbs that are easy to find in your local stores. Use this mixture to relax yourself and give your nerves a break.

TEA INGREDIENTS:
- 3 tablespoons chamomile
- 3 tablespoons peppermint
- 1 teaspoon of freshly grated ginger
- 3 ½ - 4 cups of boiling water
- Lemon slices (I normally use 2)

INSTRUCTIONS:
- Stir boiling water, chamomile, peppermint, ginger, and lemon together in a large heatproof bowl or pot.
- Allow the mixture to steep for 15 minutes.
- Strain into your cup or feel free to strain into a teapot so that it can easily be reheated.

Note: A tea ball or biodegradable empty tea bags can also be used. This tea recipe can be stored in the refrigerator for up to 3 days.

"I will not allow stress, depression or anxiety to consume me." (Affirm 3xs)

Stress, anxiety and depression can be killers; it literally means our lives to fight to rid ourselves of them. I battled with all three following my losses. As I continue to climb out of those spaces, self-talk to me includes rebuking them every time I feel them! Professional help may be the best course. I strongly encourage you to seek it. Below are some methods for coping. Choose the ones that you would like to incorporate into your life. Use this space to talk about the struggles you may have with anxiety, stress or depression. How have you managed it thus far? Have you felt like you've been suffering from one of them and have been coping by just trying to live with it?

Accept that you can't control everything
Limit your caffeine and alcohol intake (these trigger anxiety and panic attacks)
Learn to take timeouts
Identify your triggers
Use aromatherapy
Journal/Write down your thoughts
Change your diet and/or take supplements
Have a good sleep routine/get adequate rest
Stay active
Socialize and don't isolate yourself
Spend time in nature
Clean or organize your space

"I am not worthless." (Affirm 3xs)

A sad reality is that our society attaches worth to women having achieved certain milestones like being married or having children. Some are shifting away from this narrative, but it still exists. When I could not carry my first two children, I felt totally worthless. What worth could I have as a woman if I couldn't bring life into the world? I assigned my worth to things that I felt were my purpose and it was a mentally poisonous thing to do. What didn't make it better was family or friends asking me about marriage, or when I was going to have babies. It pained me to not be able to say, "I've lost the babies I wanted to have, so please choose another subject to comment about or discuss." Given the society that we live in, have you felt like there is pressure on you as a woman to be married or have children? Has family made you feel like your worth is attached to being married or having children? Have you consciously or subconsciously attached YOUR OWN worth or value to being married or having children? How do you feel about society placing such heavy value on these two things? What do you attach your value and worth to?

"I will not let my losses define me."
(Affirm 3xs)

This affirmation is one that encompasses everything in our lives, not just losing babies. We tend to keep a running list of our sufferings and allow those sufferings to become the story of who we are. This way of thinking is so unfair to us, as it allows your losses and the grief that comes from them to envelop you and put you in a space where you frequently dwell in the negative. Rewrite the story so you don't keep reliving it. Use this space to discuss your losses and reflect on what can be replaced and what cannot. Have you allowed your losses to consciously or subconsciously define you? With the losses that you cannot replace, how can you honor or grieve them to properly let them go? How can you make a conscious choice to not let your losses define you?

_____
_____
_____
_____
_____

"Relax. Breathe. Be. Everything is okay."
(Affirm 3xs)

I was in a constant state of paranoia. What would go wrong next? How bad was the worst going to be since it was always happening to me? Since such traumatic experiences happened to me, it became comfortable to assume that everything else would be like that. However, I didn't comprehend how living in that state of mind was doing nothing but attracting negativity into my life. To change my way of thinking (and essentially my reality), I intentionally planted good thoughts and practiced positive mindfulness. One of my favorite things to do at the end of the week was to write down one good thing that happened to me that week. By the end of the month I'd accumulated a handful of positive things! Short meditation and relaxation exercises also tremendously helped. Can you identify if your loss/losses has shifted you to an anxious and/or negative mind state? If you haven't consciously detected a shift, did you change in your ability to be calm, be positive or just be in the moment without needing to busy yourself? How do you ground yourself, or practice remaining in a good frame of mind?

The Womb Diaries Replenish Me, Milk & Honey Floral Bath

It's easy to find ourselves feeling depleted and drained. This luxurious bath is moisturizing and soothing, while being easy to make at home.

BATH INGREDIENTS:
- 2 cups of whole powdered milk
- 1 cup of honey powder
- ¼ cup of dried lavender
- ¼ cup of dried rose petals or rose buds
- ¼ cup dried chamomile
- ¼ cup dried calendula flowers

INSTRUCTIONS:
- Mix the powdered milk and honey powder together and then add the flowers and mix again.
- Using a small spoon or funnel, transfer your bath mixture to an airtight container. *
- To use, sprinkle ½ cup of the Replenish Me bath mixture in a warm bath. Swirl it around with your hand and enjoy!

*Note: Store this in a mason jar or other jar that has a tight-fitting lid. Honey powder draws moisture from the air if not in a sealed container. Keep in a cool, dark space.

"I make my life a celebration of their life/lives." (Affirm 3xs)

Choosing to honor your baby/babies is a good way to cope with grief. I chose to honor the babies that I lost by getting a tattoo for each of them. Anytime I get asked what the tattoos are, I always say they're for loved ones lost. The tattoos are my way of always having a piece of my children with me. There are many ways honor your children. Various jewellery pieces, creating a song playlist, holding a small memorial service, etc., are all great ways to keep their memory alive. Whatever you choose, know there is no right or wrong way to do so. All that matters is that it resonates with you. Do you choose to honor your loss/losses? If you do, what did you decide to do? If you don't do anything, would you like to? How will choosing to honor your baby/babies will help with your healing?

_____

_____

_____

_____

_____

Roleplay

A good exercise for forgiving ourselves is pretending that we are offering advice to someone who has gone through what we did. You can do this out loud or on paper. What would you say to someone to comfort them after they miscarried? What would you tell someone that blames themselves for the loss? How would you look at them? What would you tell someone that feels like they failed the baby/babies that they lost?

"Nobody nor anything can make me question my worth." (Affirm 3xs)

If I got sick, I questioned the worth of my health. If I had issues with a friend, I questioned the value of my friendship. If I had car issues, I questioned my competence. When I lost my babies, I questioned my abilities as a woman and my body. I had a habit of diminishing myself, which equated to low self-esteem. I have to actively fight to tell myself the opposite of the negative thoughts and self-talk. Self-worth is not based upon external situations. How do you define your worth? Have you ever linked your ideals of self-worth to your self-esteem? What opinions of yourself or opinions from others have influenced you? What events have occurred in your life that make you question your self-worth or hurt your self-esteem?

_____

_____

_____

_____

_____

_____

"I use my tears to water positive thoughts about myself." (Affirm 3xs)

I'm a big cry baby. I can be happy, mad, sad, frustrated, hungry, confused or whatever—I'm crying. Experiencing miscarriage had me feeling a ton of emotions and thoughts that frequently came with tears. However, in any aspect of life, we must rewire our thinking. Instead of thinking, "I feel useless because I can't do this or that," think, "I'm currently incapable of doing this or that because I don't have the knowledge of how to, yet." Instead of telling yourself, "I'd feel more beautiful if I was as skinny as her," say, "I am beautiful and will focus on changing my diet and habits to make a healthier and more attractive me." Use this space to write about some of the not-so-nice things you say or think to yourself and then restructure them to be positive.

_____
_____
_____
_____
_____

BURN IT

Grab a piece of paper and a pen. Unload all of the negativity and sadness from your loss/losses there. Unload all of the negative thoughts about yourself on that paper. Unload all of your hurt on that paper. Unleash the resentment and pain towards others on that paper. Let go of your fears on that paper. Let go of what has angered you on that paper.

Allow your higher self to guide you, and allow this outpouring to be as long or as short as it needs to be. Next, I want you to take the paper and burn it. Literally.

Burn it and watch the old you—the person you are trying to rid yourself of—be engulfed in the flames. This is a form of release.

After it burns, toss the ashes in the trash or better yet, take them outside and blow them away.

We are shedding the old skin. Tell it, "Goodbye. You are no longer welcome here."

Advancement

We move forward. You will be able to take these beginning pieces and start a new path how YOU see fit—be it via repairing relationships with others, pursuing professional help or continuing to do deeper self-help work. Perhaps you will feel a burden has been lifted after bonding with these pages and those around you. Let your intuition guide you to the course that is best for you.

"I am enough" (Affirm 3x's)

I felt like I wasn't enough or couldn't do anything right. It was as if some part of me was incomplete or faulty. Do you feel the same?

_____
_____
_____
_____
_____
_____
_____
_____
_____
_____
_____
_____

"I love you, (insert your own name here). I love myself." (Affirm 3xs)

There was an exercise that I saw online that instructed the reader to say, "I love you" to themselves in their native language throughout the course of the day. I want you to try it right now. Doesn't it feel ... weird? As strange as it may feel, affirming love to ourselves should be something that we frequently do. It's common for us to get on ourselves about the negative. Let's shift that narrative and talk about what you love about yourself. Choose some options below to give you a start and then free write to list your own.

What I love about myself:
- Sense of humor
- Laugh
- Big heart
- Love of adventure
- Loyalty
- Creativity
- Compassion
- Work Ethic
- Big heart
- Continue to love on yourself with the rest of this space.

MIRROR WORK EXERCISE

Mirror work is a very powerful tool used to help a person learn to love themselves. It helps ground you, heal your inner child, build self-confidence and overall shifts our view of ourselves. Below is a very simple mirror work exercise and you can research others that go deeper and consist of more (candles, incense, etc). To start, practice doing this exercise a few times a week for 5 minutes at a time, and gradually increase the length and frequency as you feel more comfortable and see fit.

Follow these instructions:

-Stand in front of a mirror (a handheld mirror will work if that's all you have).

-Look yourself in the eyes. Hold your gaze, even though it may be uncomfortable.

-Once you have connected with yourself, speak positive affirmations to yourself. Examples: "I love myself. I will no longer be angry. I will no longer carry sadness. I forgive myself. I am beautiful. I am strong. I am an amazing person. I am deserving of all things beautiful. I am worthy."

-After you have completed the exercise, take a deep breath and end.

"I have a healthy and beautiful body."
(Affirm 3xs)

I was angry at my body. Instead of giving it compassion and grace for enduring losses, I gave it harsh criticism and hatred. I scrutinised every physical imperfection. How foolish of me! My body, though it suffered miscarriages, had kept me alive through each of them. My body woke me up every morning, helped me move around and explore the world, and sustained me. Cursing my body was disrespectful and ungrateful of me. I had to nourish and keep it as healthy as possible. Doing anything different was essentially giving up on myself. What do people say they love about you? Is it your eyes? Your smile? What do you love about your body? Circle some (or all!) of the choices below and then write more on your own.

What I love about my body:

- Hair
- Dimples
- Legs
- Eyes
- Butt
- Freckles
- Stretch Marks

"Grieving is a necessary part of my healing." (Affirm 3xs)

Grieving was something I didn't want to do after either of my losses. It didn't necessarily feel weak, but I felt as if it was pointless. What could it change? The reality is that it couldn't change anything, but it was necessary for me. Allowing myself to mourn what was or could have been allowed that energy to be unbound from what was lost and allowed it to be placed elsewhere. Not allowing ourselves to grieve adequately keeps us tied to the past and makes it difficult to reinvest the energy that we are consciously or subconsciously holding onto. Did you allow yourself to grieve or feel as if you are still grieving? If you didn't allow yourself to grieve, why not? If you did, what did your grieving consist of? Whichever choice you made—to grieve or not to grieve—did it help?

_____
_____
_____
_____
_____

"I release all negative thoughts about myself." (Affirm 3xs)

You truly can be your own worst enemy. I had so many bad thoughts about myself, and I replayed them all day and night. They took a toll on me as I entered a state of self-loathing and self-pity. The bad thoughts had migrated from solely being about my miscarriages to other areas like my work and social life. I had to start actively changing my negative thoughts to ones that were positive. Let's take some time to do that now. Circle the things below that you love about yourself and use the extra space to write more!

What I love about myself:

- My determination
- My work ethic
- My sense of humor
- My compassion
- My heart

_____

_____

_____

The Womb Diaries Uplift My Mood Mist

Aromatherapy is so powerful! It's awesome that essential oils can be put into sprays, in diffusers, body oils and more. Try this easy blend for a quick mood booster.

SPRAY INGREDIENTS:
- 1 mini spray bottle
- ½ teaspoon of Epsom salt
- 4 ounces of distilled water
- 1 drop of eucalyptus oil
- 2 drops of geranium oil
- 3 drops of peppermint oil

INSTRUCTIONS:
- Add the Epsom salt to your spray bottle
- Add the essential oils & top with the distilled water
- Shake well before each use

"I will not listen to the thoughts and opinions of others regarding miscarriage/ early child loss." (Affirm 3xs)

Some humans can be mean. Like... REALLY MEAN. After one of my miscarriages, someone told me that I shouldn't feel that bad because I "wasn't that far along." I was livid. I overheard a conversation one day where someone said that a woman shouldn't have been sad that she lost her baby because it was still a "little blob." Yes, those were her exact words. It's disheartening how insensitive and cruel some are, but don't let those words affect you. Instead, wish for them to learn compassion and grace. What are some of the things you have heard or been told when it comes to miscarriage? Did you hear these things from those you knew? Strangers? If you knew the person that said the unkind/insensitive words, did it consciously or subconsciously change what you felt or thought about them?

_____
_____
_____
_____

"My worth is not determined by my misfortunes and losses." (Affirm 3x's)

Before I experienced my losses, I already had low self-esteem. Losing two babies made it much worse. Losing them put me in an extremely destructive self-critical mode where I thought about every single one of my mistakes, misfortunes and losses; it all made me wonder if I was really worth anything. How does your loss/losses affect your feelings of self-worth?

_____
_____
_____
_____
_____
_____
_____
_____
_____
_____

"I am not alone. I was never alone." (Affirm 3xs)

Isn't it ironic that when we're going through something, our mind makes us think that we're going through it alone? Like we are the only person that has suffered? It's an unhealthy form of thinking that can push you into isolation and depression. Unfortunately, miscarriage is very common with about 10-15 of every 100 pregnancies ending due to this devastating experience. When your loss/losses occurred, did you feel or think that you were alone? Were you scared to open up to anyone? If nobody knew you were pregnant, did that add to your feelings of loneliness? If so, how so? If others did know, did they still make you feel lonely? If so, who have you possibly, subconsciously, developed negative feelings towards because of this?

_____

_____

_____

_____

_____

"My healing heals myself, those that came before me, those that have come after me and all those that around me." (Affirm 3xs)

Healing is a beautiful thing. It's amazing to see the person we transform into when we take broken pieces and scars and build a better, stronger version of ourselves. Healing helps us break the negative and toxic cycles of those that preceded us, and allows us to start new, healthy habits and cycles for those that come after us. Healing also serves as inspiration and motivation for those around you. You are also given the chance to heal relationships around you that may have suffered intentionally or unintentionally. In terms of the loss of your baby/babies, how can your healing can help those around you, particularly in terms of understanding the experience of miscarrying in any of its forms? What relationships around you do you want to heal?

_____

_____

_____

_____

_____

"I am healing & embrace my healing process, no matter the length." (Affirm 3xs)

Healing can be so messy. It also has no time limit. It isn't linear, so you can go back and forth or up and down on any given day. When I thought I was progressing two steps in feeling better, I would get knocked back four. To this day, I am still walking the path of healing when it comes to my miscarriages. I have learned not to rush the process, but not to get stuck either. It is motivational to see the progress you make as you evolve into a new person. How has your healing process progressed? Do you feel that you started your healing process? If you didn't, can you identify how not allowing yourself to heal has negatively affected you? Do you feel as if there is no healing process that is needed for yourself?

_____
_____
_____
_____
_____
_____

BEING YOURSELF

"Be yourself, to be your best self." - Autumn Crawford

Showing up as the best version of yourself is vital to your happiness, growth and healing. Which of these do you already incorporate? Which would you like to add?

Setting boundaries
Being okay with saying "No"
Expressing my feelings
Learning when to let go
Prioritizing self-care
Taking social media breaks
Obtaining professional mental health help
Starting regular meditation
Living in a constant state of gratitude
Working on my overall health
Learning to embrace failures in a healthy manner
Practicing self-compassion
Trying new things
Rewarding myself for all wins, even small ones
Enjoying time alone
Seeking others that align with my goals
Removing the illusion of being perfect

Eliminating comparing myself to others
Asking for help when it's needed
Actively changing things I'm not happy with
Spending time out in nature

What else?

_____
_____
_____
_____
_____
_____
_____
_____
_____
_____
_____
_____
_____

"I embrace my divine feminine energy."
(Affirm 3xs)

Femininity is something that exudes from you. It can be seen and felt in your walk, your smile, how you speak, the way you govern yourself, the way you treat others and in a multitude of other ways. When I experienced my losses, I disconnected from feeling feminine because I felt less than. I'd put on the protective, rough exterior that I felt was needed to get through the traumas. I didn't have the space around me to be "soft" or vulnerable. Femininity is a gift and something I'm still actively learning to embody. It came with the reality check that I didn't really understand what it meant to be feminine. What does being feminine mean to you? Do you feel that being vulnerable is a weakness? Is being feminine something you detach from to be "strong?" Do your loss/losses make you struggle with your femininity?

_____

_____

_____

_____

_____

"I have a healthy and beautiful body." (Affirm 3x's)

I reached a point where I hated my body, and my constant battle with depression made it worse. I hated my color/shade, the size of my feet, my hair, shape of my body and even things like my nose. I had to learn to love this vessel that I've been blessed with, and to understand how to take care of it and nourish it. Our legs move us, our eyes help us see, our hands do work; our bodies are indeed beautiful! How does your loss make you feel about your body?

_____

_____

_____

_____

_____

_____

_____

_____

_____

_____

"I love, nurture and feed my body." (Affirm 3xs)

Even though I felt like my body had failed me, what I was failing to do was truly be grateful for all it had done and continued to do for me - my body sustains me as a living soul EVERYDAY! My body has navigated me into this world and will be with me for my ENTIRE LIFE. What an AMAZING vessel! As for the aches, pains and imperfections of our bodies, let's think about what we LOVE about them! Talk about how much you appreciate your body. Do you love your eyes? Or freckles? Does your body fight against or live with a disability? What ways do you currently nurture your body? What other ways can you add to nurturing your body? A workout regimen? Meditation? Better foods or adding vitamins? How about regular doctors' visits?

_____

_____

_____

_____

The Womb Diaries Luxe Bath

Ladies, let us pamper ourselves! This simple bath mixture will leave you smelling and feeling lovely. The oats, oil and salt are amazing for your skin!

BATH INGREDIENTS:
- 1 cup of dried powder milk
- 1 cup of dried rose petals and/or buds
- 20 drops of rose oil
- 25 drops of lavender oil
- 1 cup of pink Himalayan salt
- ½ of oats

INSTRUCTIONS:
- Put the salt into a bowl and add both the rose oil and lavender oil
- Allow the salt to dry
- Add and mix the rest of the ingredients to the salt

This mix makes enough for three baths. Feel free to adjust (increase or decrease) ingredients to your personal preference. Pour your mix under warm, running water, swirl with your hand and indulge yourself, Beautiful!

"I will nurture myself to be an amazing woman, friend and if I so desire... mother." (Affirm 3xs)

You can't pour from an empty cup. What good can you possibly be to anyone else if you can't even be good to yourself? As we carry on our lives with all the ebbs and flows of womanhood, it's easy to become completely depleted. When you place the weight of pregnancy issues in the mix it can feel unbearable. WE MUST nurture ourselves mind, body and soul. Journaling, staycations, spa days and working out are a few ways that we can pour back into ourselves. Below are some of the things I do to nurture and love on myself. Talk about ways you love on you and new things that you would like to incorporate.

Ways I can nurture myself:
- Meditation
- Journaling
- Dancing
- Visiting the water no matter the time of year
- Special baths (beauty/self love/rejuvenation)

_____

_____

"Life is precious & beautiful."
(Affirm 3xs)

As I move throughout the day, I make it a point to see the beauty in everything. I literally take time to gaze at the sky, flowers, the smiles of random strangers, butterflies, etc. Losing the lives that I tried to carry made me appreciate the breath that gives us on Earth, life. The more I have walked down the path of healing, the deeper my appreciation becomes for all life forces that move about this planet. The reality is we are all connected; our lives cannot exist without one another. Express what you see in your daily life that is precious and beautiful. If you need to take a break from work to step outside and get some fresh air to do this, by all means do so. What places, people or things would you like to see (near or far) that would reflect your appreciation for life?

_____

_____

_____

_____

_____

"Life is priceless to me. I treasure all life – the life I create or if I cannot create, I treasure life around me." (Affirm 3x's)

Sometimes I think we as women truly forget how powerful we are; we can literally carry and bring life into this world. For those of us that cannot carry, we are still creators and protectors. We ALL create and protect by being wives, moms, grandmothers, sisters, aunts, best friends and mentors. We have close ones that refer to us as a mother or sister figure because of the influence and weight we hold in their lives. That is precious and powerful. Suffering from loss/losses can make us lose touch with how precious life is, even if that life doesn't come directly from us. Who are some of the ones around you that you treasure and protect?

_____
_____
_____
_____
_____
_____
_____

"I will take care of myself FIRST!"
(Affirm 3xs)

How many times have we heard the saying, "You CANNOT pour from an empty cup?" When I tried to suppress the emotional and mental effects I was dealing with from the trauma of losing my babies, it took away from me taking care of myself. I neglected what I needed to internally address, and essentially it kept me from being the best version of myself. I tried to pour into work, friends, random hobbies and other things to avoid tending to my feelings and emotions. Only years later did I understand how that truly didn't help me, but I did the safest and most protective thing I knew how to do at the time. I had to learn self-awareness and self-care. What does self-care mean to you? Do you feel that your loss/losses caused you to neglect yourself intentionally or unintentionally? What forms of self-care do you take part in? What would you like to start including?

_____
_____
_____
_____

LETTER TO SELF

Now that you have navigated the waters of healing, write a letter to yourself. Fill it with forgiveness, understanding and reflection. Fill it with the goals of growth, self-repair and compassion. Think about what you may want to include. As you mend yourself, reflect on what you want to focus on moving forward for the best version of you to exist. Use as much of this space as you need.

LETTER TO SELF

LETTER TO SELF

LETTER TO SELF

To my first baby that I lost, I finally have the courage to name you. Mommy will always love you, Adam.

Dear Adam & Chloé,

I often find myself thinking about the both of you. I find myself wondering what you would've looked like, how your voices would've sounded, and what your personalities would've been like. For a long time, I felt robbed of experiencing either of you. I felt like the chance for our love was snatched away from all of us, and we were robbed of growing together. I couldn't count your new fingers and toes. I blamed myself as the reason for losing the both of you for a very long time, and it still eats away at me here and there. I will never hear you call me "Mom," but the beautiful thing is that the both of you made me a mom, even though you didn't make it here. For that, I thank you and still ask you to forgive me for not being able to safely get either of you here.

I often wonder what path life would've taken me down with either one of you, and I realize that I'm exactly where I need to be and that because of you two, I can hopefully help others who have gone through the same pain that I have. Know that you both are permanently in my heart, and I carry the strength of you two with me forever and always. Although I didn't get to meet either of you, you both immensely shaped who I am today. That is such a priceless gift. I will continue to fight to be the woman and mom that you two would've loved—the best version of myself in this human experience.

I love the both of you dearly.

From your Mommy,
Sabrina

Made in the USA
Monee, IL
23 May 2025

17715474R00069